Science Matters
THE MOON

Pat York

WEIGL PUBLISHERS INC.

Published by Weigl Publishers Inc.
123 South Broad Street, Box 227
Mankato, MN USA 56002
Web site: www.weigl.com

Library of Congress Cataloging-in-Publication Data

York, Pat, 1949-
  The moon / Pat York.
       v. cm. -- (Science matters)
Includes index.
Contents: Getting to know the moon -- What made the moon? -- The surface of the moon -- On the moon -- Map of our solar system -- Walking on the moon -- Gravity pull -- Moon time -- Surfing our solar system -- Science in action -- What have you learned?
  ISBN 1-59036-088-5 (lib. bdg. : alk. paper)
  1. Moon--Juvenile literature. [1. Moon.] I. Title. II. Series.
  QB582 .Y67 2003
  523.3--dc21
                          2002013855

Printed in the United States of America
1 2 3 4 5 6 7 8 9 0 06 05 04 03 02

Project Coordinator Jennifer Nault **Design** Terry Paulhus
Copy Editor Heather Kissock **Layout** Bryan Pezzi **Photo Researcher** Tina Schwartzenberger

Photograph Credits
Every reasonable effort has been made to trace ownership and to obtain permission to reprint copyright material. The publishers would be pleased to have any errors or omissions brought to their attention so that they may be corrected in subsequent printings.

Cover: The Moon Landing from Comstock, Inc.
Bettmann/CORBIS/MAGMA: page 15; Warren Clark: pages 12–13; COMSTOCK, Inc.: pages 3B, 7, 16; Corbis Corporation: pages 4, 17; Corel Corporation: pages 3T, 9, 10, 23T; Digital Vision: title page, pages 3M, 8, 22T, 23M, 23B; NASA: pages 6, 14, 19; Bryan Pezzi: pages 18, 21; PhotoDisc, Inc.: pages 11, 22B.

Contents

Studying the Moon

"Moon" is not only the name of Earth's nearest neighbor. It is also the name of any large object in space that circles a planet. This circular path is called an **orbit**.

Many planets have moons, and most planets have more than one moon. Earth has only one moon. The Moon is the only place in space where humans have ever landed.

■ The full Moon is the second-brightest object in the sky as seen from Earth. Only the Sun is brighter.

Moon Facts

Did you know that the Moon causes Earth's ocean tides? There are many other interesting facts about the Moon.

- The Moon is about 239,000 miles (384,633 km) away from Earth.

- The Moon is gray in color.

- The **diameter** of the Moon is about 2,160 miles (3,476 km).

- The Moon orbits Earth about every 27 days.

- The Moon's temperature is always changing. The Moon can be as cold as –280° Fahrenheit (–173°C) at night. Moon days can reach 260° Fahrenheit (127°C).

- The first unmanned landing on the Moon took place in 1959.

- Twelve people have landed on the Moon between 1969 and 1972.

The Creation of the Moon

The surface of the Moon is mostly made up of a type of rock called **basalt**. Many scientists believe that a rock called an **asteroid** struck Earth billions of years ago. They think that the asteroid chipped a large chunk off Earth. This piece of rock began to spin around Earth. It became the Moon that humans see glowing in the sky.

■ Scientists study Moon rocks. They have learned that the Moon is about 4.5 billion years old.

Moon Movement

The Moon has a special way of moving in the solar system. Read on to find out more about how the Moon moves.

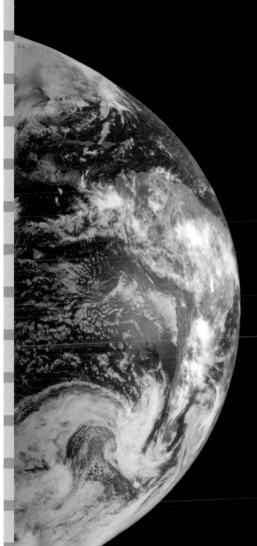

The Moon orbits Earth, and Earth orbits the Sun. A force called **gravity** keeps the Moon in its orbit around Earth. It takes the Moon about 27 days to complete one full orbit around Earth. The same part of the Moon always faces Earth. Humans must fly in spacecrafts to the Moon to see the hidden part.

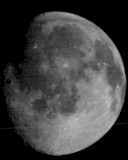

The Moon's Surface

Dark spots can be seen on the Moon on a moonlit night. The dark spots are low, flat areas called *maria*. *Maria* means "seas" in Latin. Brighter areas are called highlands. They are rugged mountains and plains.

Round holes dot the Moon. They are called craters. Craters are formed when asteroids crash into the Moon's surface.

■ There are more than 3 trillion craters on the Moon.

Moon Time

Did you know that all calendars are not the same? The calendar that is used every day is based on the Sun. There is also a calendar based on the Moon.

A year on our calendar lasts 365 days. This is how long it takes Earth to orbit the Sun. Still, this is not the only calendar that exists. Some people use a **lunar** calendar. It is based on the **phases** of the Moon. A lunar year has 354 days. Twelve lunar months make a lunar year. The Muslim and Jewish religions use lunar calendars. The lunar calendar is also used to mark the dates of Chinese festivals and holidays. For instance, the Chinese New Year follows the lunar calendar.

On the Moon

There is no air on the Moon. Sound needs air to travel. This means that there is also no sound on the Moon. If a person shouted on the Moon, there would be no noise.

The temperature on the Moon is very hot during the day. The Moon is extremely cold at night. The Moon does not have wind or rain because there is no air or water. Wind is moving air, and rain is falling water.

■ Most **astronomers** believe the Moon has no water. Still, some think the Moon's north and south poles have ice.

A Moonlight Experiment

Did you know that the Moon does not create its own light? Try this experiment to discover why the Moon can be seen from Earth.

The Moon appears to glow because it **reflects** the light of the Sun. Sunlight shines onto the surface of the Moon and is bounced off. The Moon's glow is actually caused by sunlight.

Learn about reflection using a flashlight. You will need a partner for this experiment. First, find a dark room. Next, shine a flashlight onto your partner's face. Do you notice how the light shines off your partner's face? It is reflecting the light from the flashlight. This is how the Moon reflects the Sun's light.

Solar System Map

Match each planet on the left to its orbit in the diagram. This will show you the order of the planets in our solar system.

- Mercury
- Venus
- Earth
- Mars
- Jupiter
- Saturn
- Uranus
- Neptune
- Pluto

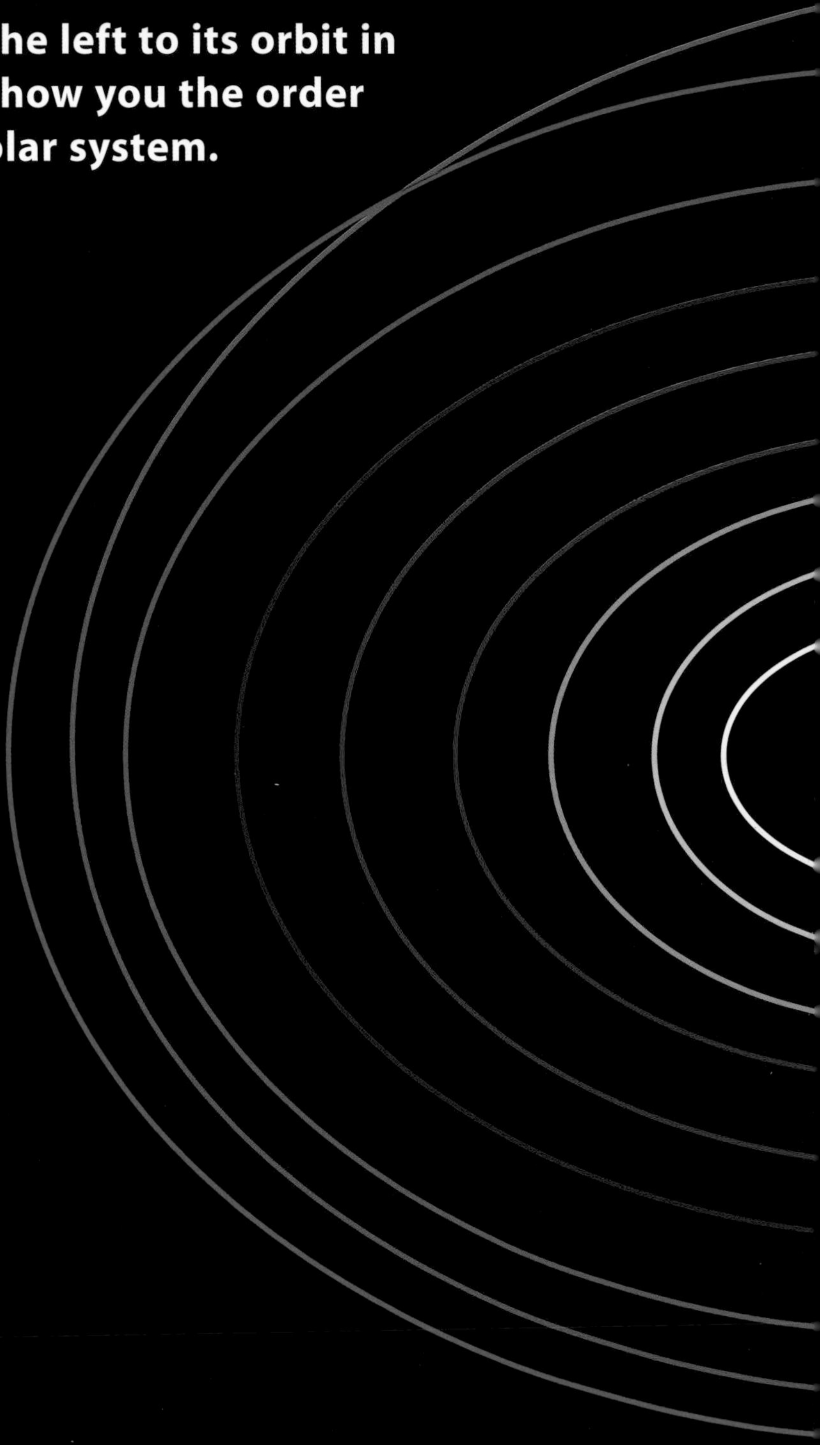

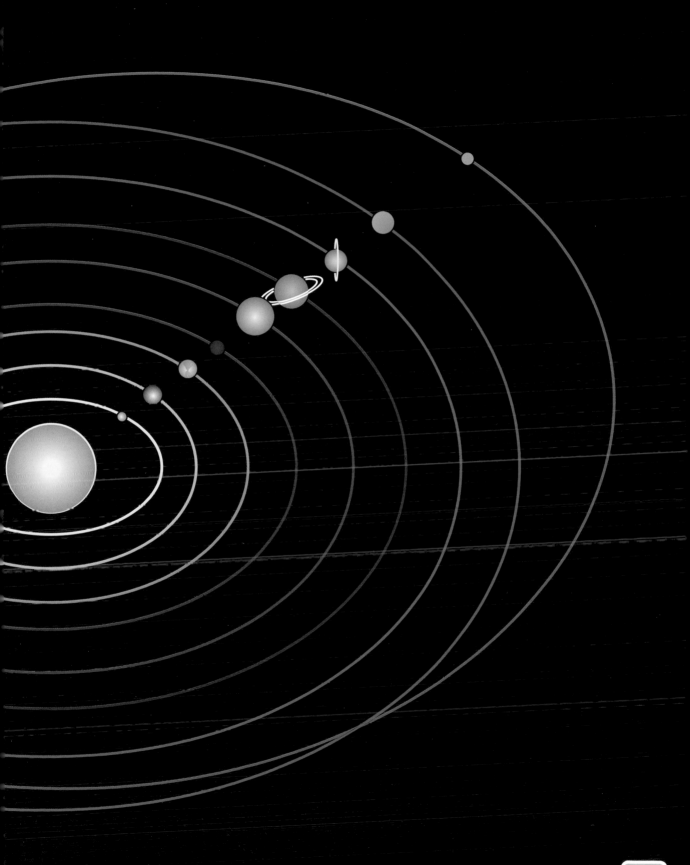

Walking on the Moon

Astronauts Neil Armstrong and Buzz Aldrin landed on the Moon on July 20, 1969. They flew to the Moon on board the *Apollo 11*. They took photographs of the Moon's surface. Before the astronauts left, they placed a sign that read, "We Came in Peace for all Mankind." Rocks and bags of soil were brought back to Earth.

■ Buzz Aldrin stepped onto the Moon 20 minutes after Neil Armstrong's first step. Buzz collected rock samples.

The First Step

Neil Armstrong was the first person to walk on the Moon. Many more voyages to the Moon have been made since that first visit.

Neil Armstrong traveled to the Moon on board the *Apollo 11*, a spaceship. Neil carried a camera to record his first steps on the Moon. Many people watched him on television. During his moonwalk, Neil Armstrong said: "That's one small step for man, one giant leap for mankind."

Gravity's Pull

Earth's gravity is six times stronger than the Moon's gravity. This means that the Moon's gravity has less force, or pull, than the Earth's gravity. People are much lighter on the Moon than they are on Earth. Spacesuits are also lighter. A 220-pound (100 kg) spacesuit weighs about 36 pounds (16 kg) on the Moon.

■ Astronauts can jump very high and leap very far on the Moon.

A Gravity Experiment

Become an astronaut for a day. This activity will show you how the Moon's gravity feels.

The Moon's gravity is much weaker than Earth's. This fun experiment will show you how light objects feel on the Moon.

You will need:
- two 1-gallon (3.8 L) jugs
- a measuring cup
- water

Fill one jug up to the top with water. Tighten the lid. Next, measure 2.5 cups (591 ml) of water. Pour the water into the second jug and tighten the lid.

Go outside to an open area. Throw the first jug as far as possible. Next, throw the second jug. The lighter jug should travel much farther. This is how Moon gravity affects astronauts.

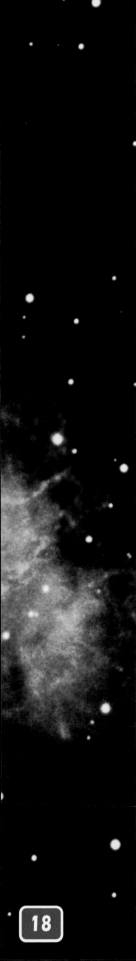

Moon Phases

The Sun shines on different parts of the Moon as the Moon orbits Earth. Sometimes, the far side of the Moon is lit, and the side closest to Earth is dark. This is called a new Moon. The sky is very dark during a new Moon.

The Moon and Earth are always moving. This means that the Sun shines on a different part of the Moon every night. The changes in the way the Moon appears from Earth are called Moon phases.

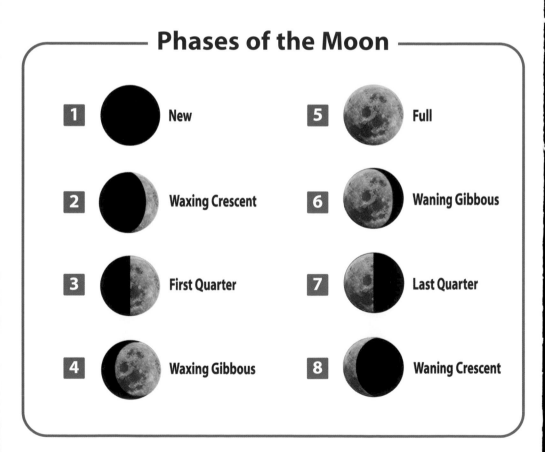

Phases of the Moon

1	New	5	Full
2	Waxing Crescent	6	Waning Gibbous
3	First Quarter	7	Last Quarter
4	Waxing Gibbous	8	Waning Crescent

■ The Moon goes through eight phases. It takes more than 29 days for the Moon to go through all of the phases.

A Moon Story

The Inuit people tell a story about the Moon. Their Moon god is named *Anningan*. Their Sun goddess is called *Malina*.

Anningan likes to chase his sister, Malina, in circles. Sometimes, Anningan is so busy chasing Malina that he forgets to eat. When this happens, he becomes a crescent Moon. Anningan goes away for a moment to eat. He becomes a new Moon while he is gone. Soon, Anningan begins to get fatter and rounder. He is called a full Moon when he is completely round.

Anningan never stops chasing Malina. The story is meant to explain why the phases of the Moon repeat forever.

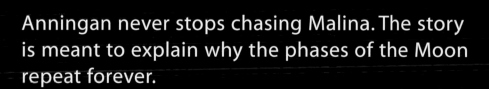

Surfing Our Solar System

How can I find more information about space?
- Libraries have many interesting books about space.
- Science centers are great places to learn about space.
- The Internet offers some great Web sites dedicated to space.

Where can I find a good reference Web site to learn more about space?
Encarta Homepage
www.encarta.com
- Type any space-related term into the search engine. Some terms to try include "asteroid" and "galaxy."

How can I find out more about space, rockets, and astronauts?
NASA Kids
http://kids.msfc.nasa.gov
- This Web site offers puzzles and games, along with the latest news on NASA's research.

Science in Action

Moon Tale

Make up your own story about the Moon. Give the Moon a different name. Explain in your story why the Moon seems to be following the Sun.

Create a Moon Calendar

Find an empty calendar with large squares. Watch the Moon and record the shape it takes for 30 days. Each night, draw the shape of the Moon on the calendar. It may seem like the Moon's shape is not changing at first. Soon, you will see that the Moon's shape has changed. You will have drawn all of the Moon's phases by the end of the month.

October

Sun	Mon	Tues	Wed	Thur	Fri	Sat
1 New Moon	2	3	4 Waxing Crescent	5	6	7
8	9 First Quarter	10	11	12	13 Waxing Gibbous	14
15	16	17 Full Moon	18	19	20	21 Waning Gibbous
22	23	24	25 Last Quarter	26	27	28
29 Waning Crescent	30	31				

What Have You Learned?

1. Is Earth the only planet with a Moon?

2. What color is the Moon?

3. What do we call the different shapes of the Moon as seen from Earth?

4. Can all parts of the Moon be seen from Earth?

5. Does the Moon make its own light?

6 Who were the first humans to walk on the Moon?

7 Is the gravity on the Moon the same force as the gravity on Earth?

8 What do the Inuit people call the Moon? What do they call the Sun?

9 How many days are there in a lunar calendar?

10 Do humans weigh more on the Moon or on Earth?

Answers: 1. No. Most planets have more than one moon. **2.** Gray **3.** Phases **4.** No. Only one side of the Moon faces Earth. **5.** No. The Moon reflects the Sun's light. **6.** Neil Armstrong and Buzz Aldrin **7.** No. Earth's gravity is six times stronger. **8.** The Moon is called *Anningan* and the Sun is called *Malina*. **9.** 354 **10.** Humans weigh much more on Earth.

Words to Know

asteroid: a small, solid object in space that circles the Sun

astronomers: people who study space and its objects

basalt: a hard rock formed in very hot conditions

diameter: the measurement of a straight line passing through the center of a circle

gravity: a force that pulls things toward the center

lunar: related to the Moon

orbit: the circular path a planet makes around an object in the sky, such as the Sun

phases: the appearance of the Moon from Earth

reflects: throws or bends light back

Index